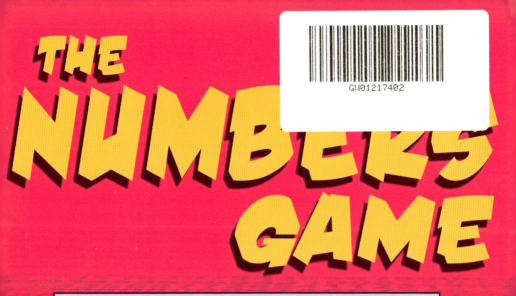

THE NUMBERS GAME

Numbers are all around us and we use them every day. This booklet is designed to show that maths doesn't have to be scary and you don't have to take it too seriously. This is a book about maths - it's not a maths book!

There is lots to do here, hopefully involving various members of the family. In case some of you want a bit more information, Matthew Mattick has given some added details. He looks a dumb kid but is actually an undiscovered genius. He also loves corny gags and jokes - so we let him put in a few of those too. He's got a cat called Digit and a pet mouse called Fraction.

We hope you have lots of fun with the book.

Fraction | Digit | Matthew Mattick

ARE YOU AS LONG AS YOU ARE WIDE?

Stretch your arms out and measure the length from fingertip to fingertip (your arm span). Then compare this to the length of your body. Do it with other members of the family. What do you find?

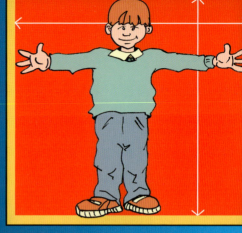

MATTHEW MATTICK SAYS...

Mathematicians and philosophers measured the human body to see if they could discover anything about the laws nature. Leonardo da Vinci was a mathematician as well as an artist and he made this famous drawing of the proportions of the body. Lucky about the fig leaf, eh?

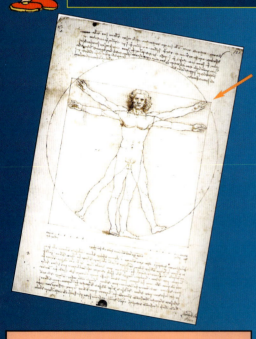

WILL YOU TAKE £1 MILLION?

You've just won a special prize in a competition. You can have either £1 million now or you can have 1p today, double the amount tomorrow and double each day for 30 days. Which will you take? Try to work out how much you will get after 30 days. Were you right in your choice?

WHO WAS THE FIRST MATHS STUDENT?
ADD-EM (ADAM)!

P-S-S-S-ST Matthew! There's a man behind me holding up a card with a number on it...

Yes Digit. That's the **page numbers**. Now please don't bother me, I have to go to page 3 to look at some jellybeans!!

FOR RICHER OR POORER

Would you rather become 50% richer and then 50% poorer, or 50% poorer and then 50% richer? Is there any difference?

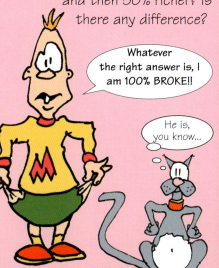

ESTIMATING AND COUNTING

Find reasons to estimate and count things - grapes in a bunch, coins in your hand, number of slices you have cut a banana into. You estimate too and explain how you made your guess.

MORE ESTIMATING

Wrap up a variety of things and ask your child to put them in order from lightest to heaviest. Check the weights then on kitchen or bathroom scales.

How many steps to cross a room? Or guess how many centimetres or metres in length something is. Check to see how accurate you have been. When on a walk, guess how many steps from one lamp post to another. Who won? Try the best of three guesses.

Guess how full a cereal box is by weighing it in their hands. Check before pouring out. Before you go shopping, send your child to see how much milk you've got and ask him to decide if the milk bottle is half full, quarter full etc.

How long has it taken / will it take to complete a task? How long will a journey take?
How many tiles on the bathroom wall?
How much will the shopping cost?
Which container will hold the most water?

CODE GAME

All you need to be able to send a secret message to someone is a piece of paper, a pen or pencil and a secret code.

As long as the sender and receiver of the message both have the same code, and no-one else does, the message will stay secret.

A simple way to code is called a **substitution code**, where instead of writing a letter, you write a number followed by a dot or a zero. So instead of "a" you write "1." or "10"

Write out the whole code twice on two separate pieces of paper. Give one to the person you're sending a message to, and keep one yourself. Write your message out below the code. Then on a new piece of paper, write the coded message, and send it to your friend or family member. Your message will stay secret as long as no-one else gets hold of the code!

MATTHEW MATTICK SAYS...

The proper name for a coded message is a **cryptogram**. These have been used for over 2500 years, usually during wars when it is important that the enemy doesn't know what you are planning to do next. The most famous code-breaking story is that of the ENIGMA code in World War two.

CRYPTIC CODES

A=1	A=O	A=m
B=2	B=P	B=r
C=3	C=Q	C=b
D=4	D=R	D=f
E=5	E=S	E=s
F=6	F=T	F=l
G=7	G=U	G=w
H=8	H=V	H=t
I=9	I=W	I=e
J=10	J=X	J=c
K=11	K=Y	K=n
L=12	L=Z	L=x
M=13	M=A	M=z
N=14	N=B	N=u
O=15	O=C	O=i
P=16	P=D	P=y
Q=17	Q=E	Q=v
R=18	R=F	R=o
S=19	S=G	S=g
T=20	T=H	T=j
U=21	U=I	U=q
V=22	V=J	V=a
W=23	W=K	W=h
X=24	X=L	X=p
Y=25	Y=M	Y=k
Z=26	Z=N	Z=d
SPACE = /		

Above are three codes: a number substitutions code, an offset substitution code, and a random substitution code. Write out the coding and decoding lists separately, in alphabetical order, to make coding and decoding easier; (don't get muddled up!). Try making up a code of your own or code the message twice over using the same list (needs double decoding).

SECRET MESSAGE 1

20.15 / 13.25 /
2.18.15.20.8.5.18.
25.15.21.18 / 16.15.3.11.5.20 /
13.15.14.5.25'19 / 7.15.14.5 /
19.16.5.14.20 / 9.20 / 1.12.12
15.14 /
19.23.5.5.20.19 /
6.15.18 / 13.5.

I think I've got a code!

SECRET MESSAGE 1 - REPLY

(decoding is right to left on the code list shown)

e'z bizeuw uih gi xsw ej vqebn.
e tiys jtigs ghssjg hexx zmns
kiq gebn.

MATCH CHALLENGES

Arrange 9 matchsticks in this shape:

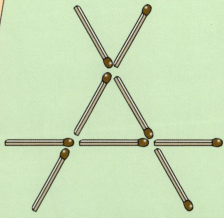

Now move 4 matchsticks to make 5 triangles.

Arrange 12 matches like this:

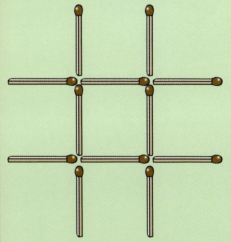

Can you move 4 to make 3 equal squares that are all connected?

ON THE ROAD

Let's see who can **find 10 red cars** first.

Licence plate game - find the number 1 on a licence plate, then 2, 3 and so on. Whoever gets to 9 first wins. You could extend it by including the numbers 10, 11 etc., together.

Ralph: Dad, will you do my maths for me tonight?
Dad: No, son, it wouldn't be right.
Ralph: Well, you could try.

"Excuse me, Russian Peasant stereotype, but would you mind awfully multiplying **22 by 44**?"

"**968**! Iz eazy! Peasant method iz good, no? (You like rabbit stew?)"

RUSSIAN MULTIPLICATION

Russian peasants used an interesting way of multiplying large numbers. For example, if the numbers are 22 x 44, you halve one number and double the other, ignoring any remainders.

Where the number in the halve column is odd, including the original number, you should repeat the number that is in the double column in the add column. Add up these numbers. In this example the total is 968. It sounds totally scary but look at the example and you'll see how easy it is!

Draw three columns and label them.

Write the numbers to be multiplied. **Halve** column is an even number so the **Add** column stays empty.

Halve column one, Double column two. The **Halve** number is odd so put the number in **Double** column into **Add** column also. Repeat this for the third line.

Halve column one, Double column two. The **Halve** number is now even so no number goes in the **Add** column.

Halve one and Double two as before. The **Halve** number is odd so the **Double** number goes in the **Add** column also.

Add the Add column to get the answer.

Halve	Double	Add
22	44	
11	88	88
5	176	176
2	352	
1	704	704
		968

Try one for yourself: 25 x 34.

What's a polygon? A dead parrot!

COLOUR PUZZLE

In 1852 a mathematician called Francis Guthrie suggested that any map could be coloured using just 4 colours and that no two countries next to each other need have the same colour. This became known as the Four Colour Problem and wasn't solved until 1976, with the help of a huge computer.

Trace over the puzzle first and then see if you can do this puzzle. No two sections that touch can be the same colour and you can only use 4 colours. (Hint: start from the middle and work out).

GAME OF 15

You will need paper and pens. Game for 2 players.
Write the numbers 1 2 3 4 5 6 7 8 9 on a piece of paper. The aim is to choose any **3** numbers that add up to 15. Take it in turns to select a number and then cross that number out - it can't be used again. The first player to have any 3 numbers that add up to 15 wins.

Example:
Player 1 chooses 8
Player 2 chooses 6
Player 1 chooses 4
Player 2 chooses 3 (to stop Player 1 getting 8+4+3)
Player 1 chooses 9
Player 2 chooses 2
Player 1 chooses 1
Player 2 chooses 7 (Now has 6+2+7=15)

Right! I'm off to get my crayon set with four colours in it!

Erk! I had those last week and broke all the points off.

And I threw them out of the window!

Q: Why didn't the two 4s want any dinner?
A: Because they already 8!

DICE FOOTBALL

All you need is a dice, paper and pen. League tables are very important to football clubs and fans because they show how the team is doing compared with other teams in the division, and at the end of the season which team will win the title, which are promoted and relegated. Select four teams. Each team will play the others, home and away. On a piece of paper, draw a chart like the one below, to record your results. Role the dice for each team and record the score.

Using your results, fill in a league table like the one below.

P - Played; W - Won; D - Drawn; L - Lost; F - Goals for; A - Goals against; GD - Goal Difference (F minus A); Pts - Points. 3 points for a win, 1 point for a draw, no points for a loss.

RESULTS SHEET

Team	Team Name	Dice score	vs	Team	Team Name	Dice score
1	Manchester United	1		2	Exeter City	5
3				4		
1				3		
2				4		
4				1		

LEAGUE TABLE

Team	P	W	D	L	F	A	GD	Pts
Exeter City	6	4	1	1	17	9	8	13

288!

Disgusting!

Q: Why can't you say 288 in public?
A: It's two gross!

ONE TO NINE

Copy the diagram below. Using all the numbers 1 to 9, complete the triangle so that when you add up all the numbers on each side of the triangle, they equal 20.

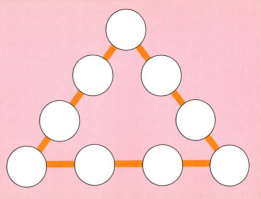

ONE TO NINE AGAIN

Using all the numbers 1 to 9, fill in the circles so that each line of circles adds up to 18.

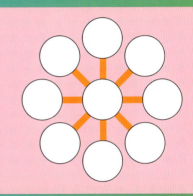

SUM TRICK THIS

Ask someone to add these numbers up in their head...

1000
Add 10
Add 1000
Add 20
add 1000
add 30
add 1000
add 40

What do you get? (The answer is not 5000!)

Q: Why was the maths book sad?
A: Because it had too many problems.

GEOMETRIC SHAPES

square, circle, rectangle, triangle, sphere, cube, cone, pyramid, cylinder, octagon, pentagon, heptagon, hexagon, triangular prism, triangular-based prism, rectangular prism, rectangular-based prism.

See how many shapes you can find in your house or on a walk.

Luckily, I do actually have a little eye to spy with!

sphere

cone

pyramid

SHAPE I-SPY

Take it in turns to say, "I spy with my little eye, something that is....." Square shaped, round shaped, spherical, cube shaped etc. You can play this anywhere of course.

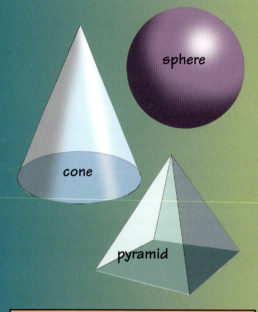

Q: If you had 3 apples and 4 oranges in one hand and 3 apples and 3 oranges in other hand, what would you have?
A: Very Large Hands

square

circle

rectangle

triangle

parallelogram

octagon

IMAGINE A SHAPE

Close your eyes and imagine there is a cube in front of you. See it in your mind. How many faces (sides) does it have? How many corners? How many edges? Seeing shapes in your head is very important in maths.

PALINDROMIC NUMBERS

A palindrome is a word which spells the same forwards and backwards - words like dad, kayak, madam. A palindromic number is one that reads the same forward or backward, such as 55, 828, 2992. If a number is not already palindromic, you can make it so by adding its reverse and repeating until it is palindromic. For example:

```
              731
+ its reverse 137
              868
```

Sometimes you have to carry on for a lot longer.

```
              398
+ its reverse 893
             1291
+ its reverse 1921
             3212
+ its reverse 2123
             5335
```

Now work out the palindromic numbers for 338, 69 and 89 (this one will test you out!)

cube

Well Fraction, a palindrome is a sort of aerodrome, but with Michael Palin in it. (I think..?)

Stupid cat...!

MATTHEW MATTICK SAYS...

Palindromes exist in word and letter form too. For example "Mr Owl ate my metal worm" or "Able I was ere I saw Elba". Palindromes that make no sense can be hundreds of words long.

MAGIC SQUARES
Draw the squares out on a piece of paper.

Use the numbers 1 to 9.
Each line should add up to 15.

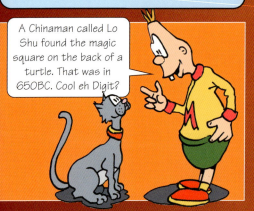

Use only the even numbers from 2 to 18.
Each line should add up to 30.

That boy's mind is in **turtle chaos!**

Use only odd numbers from 1 to 17.
Each line should add up to 27.

Q: How many seconds are there in a year?
A: 12 (January 2nd, February 2nd....)

12

	5	

	10	

	9	

MAKE A RAIN GAUGE

You will need: scissors, a plastic bottle.

Cut the bottle one third from the top, so you have two pieces. (Take the lid off first). Turn the top part upside down and push it into the bottom part.

Put the bottle outside and using a plastic ruler, measure how much rain you collect each week.

You could make a chart to show how much it rains for a week, or a month.

1	2	3	4
5	6	7	8
9	10	11	12

COVER UP

A game for 2 players. You will need paper and pen and 2 dice. Draw two grids the same as the one above. Each player has one grid. Players take it in turn to throw the 2 dice. After throwing, the player may either do nothing or cover up the number or numbers that exactly add up to the total of the two dice. So, if the dice numbers are 2 and 4, you can cover up those numbers on your grid. If they are already covered, you could cover 6, or 1 and 5. The winner is the first player to cover up all numbers on his grid.

Rain in June and July

There are three kinds of mathematicians: those who can count and those who cannot.

MURDER AT THE ..... HOLIDAY LODGE

There has been a murder at the Holiday Lodge. You've been sent to solve it. The Holiday Lodge has four rooms. At the time of the murder, the four suspects and the four weapons were each in a different room.

There are ten pieces of information that are known to be fact.

- **Major Blunder** was in the kitchen.
- **Mr Point** was in the same room as the carving knife
- The gun was in the dining room
- The murder wasn't committed in the lounge
- Neither of the male suspects was in a room next to the kitchen
- The victim was not shot.
- **Ms Took** was not in the same room as the gun
- The rat poison was not in the kitchen
- **Mrs Lacking** was not in the room next door to where the murder was committed.
- The Major is innocent.

This is a plan of the lodge

| Kitchen | Hall |
| Dining Room | Lounge |

Using the information above and the logic tables below, find out: Who committed the murder? Where? With which weapon?

	Bat	Knife	Gun	Poison
Hall				
Kitchen				
Diningroom				
Lounge				

	Bat	Knife	Gun	Poison
Blunder				
Point				
Took				
Lacking				

	Hall	Kitchen	Diningroom	Lounge
Blunder				
Point				
Took				
Lacking				

Q: Why was six afraid of seven? A: Because 7 ATE 9!

NEW FOOTBALL STRIP

The players in a mixed Under 11 football squad are being given new shirts with their numbers on. But they aren't told the numbers - they have to work them out from clues. Can you give a number to each player in the squad?

Josh's and Andy's numbers add up to 19. Their numbers multiplied together is 84. What are their numbers?

Lucy, Rachel, Suha, Randeep and Stefan will wear consecutive numbers and the average is 4. What are their numbers?

Micky and Chris have numbers that add up to 21. The numbers have a difference of 5. What are their numbers?

Sonia's number is double Aasim's and the two numbers add up to 27. Will's number is one less than Leanne's and Finn's number is 6 more than Will's. Leanne's number is the same as Randeep's and Stefan's added together.

THE MÖBIUS STRIP

Cut a strip of paper about 300mm long and 40mm wide.
Bring the ends together, but twist it once before sticking the ends together with quick-stick glue.

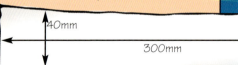

This shape only has one side! Prove it by colouring one side all the way round - you'll end up where you started from. There is NO OTHER SIDE. It has only got one edge too!

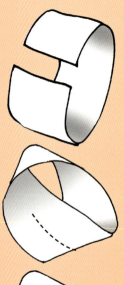

It gets better: take some scissors and cut it in half as shown. See what happens.

Make up another strip, but this time cut it one third of the way across as shown. See what happens now. Guaranteed to amaze!

MATTHEW MATTICK SAYS...

No-one would have remembered August Möbius if he hadn't discovered this strange shape in 1858. Mathematicians who study shapes are called topologists and Möbius was by all accounts a very boring topologist. The Möbius strip, though, is a real wonder - maybe the only glimpse that most of us will ever have into such a strange and difficult field of mathematics.

SPIDERS

You will need a piece of paper and pens.

Choose a number - between 5 and 20. Write the number in the middle of the paper. Take turns to draw lines from the number and write down a sum that equals the number in the middle. For example:

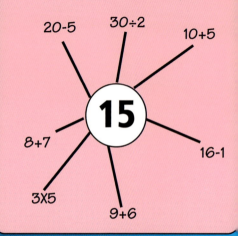

What did the maths book say to his troubled friend?
Sorry, I can't help you; I've got too many problems of my own!

FOLDING PAPER

Take a piece of paper. Fold it in half. Do this 7 more times.

Having trouble? You're not the first. All would be fine if the paper was thin enough and had no mechanical properties. The number of layers of paper in your folded piece starts at 1.

First fold gives you 2, second fold gives you 4, third = 8, 4th = 16, 5th = 32, 6th = 64, 7th = 128 and 8th = 256. It's not just the doubling effect though. Mathematicians have pondered this problem in depth and they think they have finally worked out why you can't do it. The real answer is that it's too difficult - why should we want to know more than that?

Powerful magnifying glass!

I take the paper, and I fold it...

I take the paper, and I fold it...

I take the paper, and I fold it...

I take the paper, and I fold it...

MATTHEW MATTICK SAYS...

If you take a number, double it, then keep doubling it, you are going to get very big numbers in a very short time. Bacteria reproduce by each of them dividing in half - literally by doubling themselves. They do this each 20 minutes or so. In 24 hours, one single solitary bacillus can double itself 72 times over - so there'd be 4,722,366,482,800,000,000,000 of them. Lucky they're small! Crikey! I think I've just told you how to be a millionaire (see page 2).

and as you can't see me now, I have thrown the paper away. Impossible!

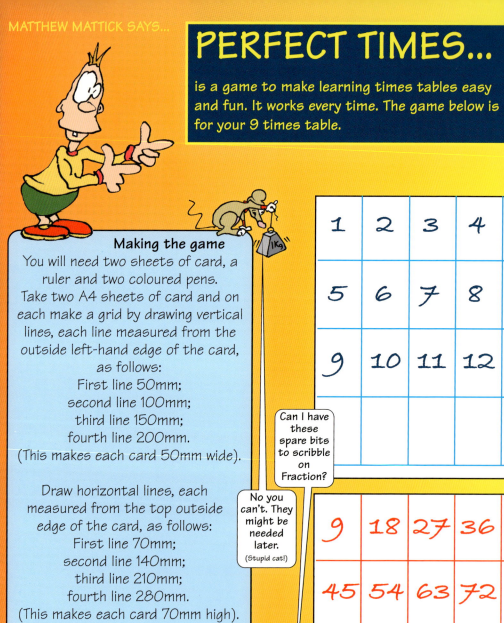

MATTHEW MATTICK SAYS...

PERFECT TIMES...

is a game to make learning times tables easy and fun. It works every time. The game below is for your 9 times table.

Making the game

You will need two sheets of card, a ruler and two coloured pens. Take two A4 sheets of card and on each make a grid by drawing vertical lines, each line measured from the outside left-hand edge of the card, as follows:
First line 50mm;
second line 100mm;
third line 150mm;
fourth line 200mm.
(This makes each card 50mm wide).

Draw horizontal lines, each measured from the top outside edge of the card, as follows:
First line 70mm;
second line 140mm;
third line 210mm;
fourth line 280mm.
(This makes each card 70mm high).

Cut out the cards. There will be two sets of cards and 16 cards in each set. One set will be the FACTOR cards, showing the numbers 1 to 12. The second set will be the MULTIPLES, or answer cards.

Can I have these spare bits to scribble on Fraction?

No you can't. They might be needed later.
(Stupid cat!)

18

For the 9 times table, this will be the numbers 9, 18, 27, 36 and so on. You will have 4 spare cards in each set.

On your Factor cards write the numbers 1,2,3,4,5,6,7,.8,9,10,11,12 boldly in the centre of the card. Leave the spare ones blank - you can use them if you lose any of the cards.

On your Multiple cards write the numbers 9,18,27,36,45,54,63,72,81,90,99,108 in the centre of the cards in a different colour. Leave the spares blank.

Playing Times Up

Shuffle up the Multiple cards and place them on a flat surface in a 3 x 4 grid, as shown opposite. Shuffle up the Factor cards and, playing them in the order they appear, match the multiple card to the right factor card. For example, the number 6 will go on top of 54. As you make the match say the table fact out loud - 6 x 9 is 54. It's best if you can time yourself, or get someone else to time you. When you've finished, check the answers are correct. Then shuffle up the multiple cards again, and the factor cards and play again. See if you can beat your time. Try to do the nine times table in under 20 seconds. You could make two sets and have competitions in the family.

27	99	36	108
45	9	63	54
72	18	81	90

Have you noticed that all the answers (multiples) add up to 9? Also have you noticed that the multiple card starts with one number less than the factor? So 7 x 9; the answer will start with 6 (7-1) and will add up to 9, so the second number must be 3.

You can make other times tables in the same way, or you can buy a full set of **Perfect Times**, with instructions about other games you can play. Go to **www.southgatepublishers.co.uk**

FUN WITH CALCULATORS

WHEN WERE YOU BORN?

Here is a way to work out when someone was born.

Using a calculator, ask someone to put in the day of the month they were born. So if it was October 28th 1998, they enter 28. Ask the person to multiply by 20, add 3 and multiply by 5. Then add the number of the month they were born (in this case 10), multiply by 20, add 3 and multiply by 5. Then ask him to add on the last two numbers of the year he was born (98). Take the calculator from him and subtract 1515. You can then read out the person's date of birth - 281098.

Using a calculator, enter 4240. Divide by 0.4, add 9 and multiply by 5. Turn the calculator upside down. What word can you see?

Grandad was born in 1958 (key in). Add his height (170 cm), divide by his weight (76 kg), add his shoe size (9) and divide by his house number (100). Turn the calculator upside down. What is his name? Make up some of your own!

This is DOUG MATTICK (Matthew's opinionated Grandpappy. It's his nickname you're working out above.

This is KERIS MATTICK (Matthew's wonderful little niece).

I don't believe in this, and I don't believe in that either

gerblumblediddly e=mc² ooo poop

parp!

Q: What does the little mermaid wear?
A: An Algebra

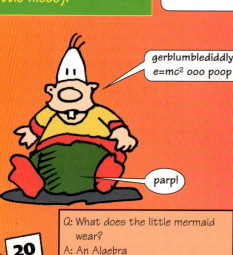

I CAN READ YOUR MIND!

Ask a friend to think of a number and write it down on a piece of paper, without letting you see it. Give her a calculator and tell her to: enter the number, double it, add 4, divide by 2, add 7, multiply by 8, subtract 12, divide by 4, subtract 11. Now, take the calculator yourself, subtract 4 from the number shown and divide by 2. The answer will be the original number.

MATTHEW MATTICK SAYS...

In 1948 a brilliant mathematician called Alan Turing invented a new type of computing machine which was to set the design standards for all computers since. It was built in Manchester and took up all the space in three large rooms at the university's physics department. Although the principle is the same today as it was then, the components of computers have been made smaller and smaller until we can all have the power of Turing's computer (and more) in a tiny plastic case. The hand held calculator allows us to do complicated calculations hundreds of times quicker than we could with pen and paper.

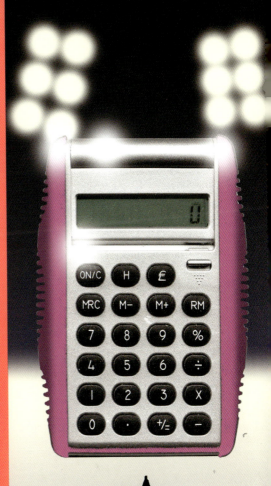

Matthew, I thought you said that a modern calculator was a very small thing?

It is Digit, but this display symbolises its importance in our lives...

...or maybe it's just for people with big problems?

Birds on the mountain,
Fish in the sea,
How you passed maths
Is a mystery to me.

BILLY GOATS GRUFF CHALLENGE

Once upon a time there lived three goats. Their names were; Trip, Trap and Trop. The three goats enjoyed eating and happily munched their way through all of the grass on their side of the river. When the grass started to run out, the goats panicked.
"What are we going to do?" grumbled Trip.
We have to find a way to get to the other side of the river, there's lots of tasty green grass over there," explained Trap.
The goats spent days trying to think of how to get across the river as there was a bit of a problem.

Over the river was a bridge, but the bridge was guarded by an evil troll who would gobble them up, so they had to find another way. There was a boat but unfortunately the boat was not very strong so would not be able to take them all together at the same time. Also, the goats had to take with them their pets because they couldn't live without them.

"I've got to take my snake," cried Trip.
"I've got to take my mouse," shouted Trap.
"And I've got to take my hawk," stamped Trop.

The boat could only take one or two creatures at a time, so two goats could go or a goat and a pet. Now we all know, snakes eat mice and hawks eat snakes, so these creatures cannot be left alone together unless they have a goat with them watching. Also the pet cannot go on the boat without its owner.

Can you help the goats because without you they will not get to eat the tasty grass across the river? Plan a safe route that means all of the goats and all of the pets get across safely without any of them being eaten. Try to do it in the least number of trips for the boat.

Story from **Tales with a Twist**, (Southgate)

I AM NOT GOING ANYWHERE NEAR **THEM**

NUMBER HANGMAN

You will need paper and pencil. Think of a sum, eg **2315+427**.
Write down:

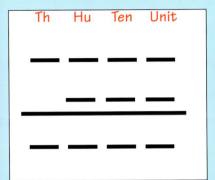

Play Hangman

The object of the game is to work out the sum before the hangman is completed. Children ask questions like, **"Are there any 9s in the tens column?"** In this case there aren't so you draw the first part of the hangman.

Why did the man sleep with a ruler?
To see how long he could sleep.

Answers:

Page 2
As long as wide - approx the same.
Will you take a million - take 1p (over £5million!).

Page 3
Richer or poorer - they are the same.

Page 4
Secret message 1 - TO MY BROTHER. YOUR POCKET MONEY'S GONE YOU SEE, I'VE SPENT IT ALL ON SWEETS FOR ME.
Reply: I'M COMING NOW SO LEG IT QUICK. I HOPE THOSE SWEETS WILL MAKE YOU SICK.

Page 5
Match Challenges.

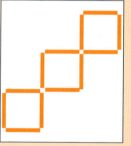

Page 6
25 x 34 = 850.

H	D	A
25	34	34
12	68	-
6	136	-
3	272	272
1	544	544
		850

Page 7

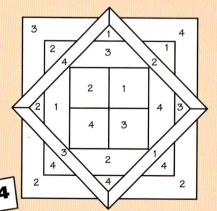

Page 9

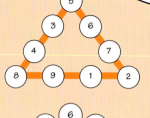
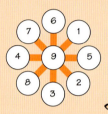

Sum Trick This - 4100

Page 11
Palindromic numbers:
338 - 2882
69 - 4884
89 - 8813200023188

Page 12
Magic squares

8	3	4
1	5	9
6	7	2

16	6	8
2	10	18
12	14	4

15	5	7
1	9	17
11	13	3